SEXUAL ENERGY
TRANSMUTATION

SEXUAL ENERGY TRANSMUTATION
Copyright © 2012 Jay Onwukwe
All rights reserved.

ISBN-13:978-1477474143
ISBN-10:   1477474145

The information contained in this book is intended to be educational and not for diagnosis, prescription or treatment of any health disorder whatsoever. The author and publisher are not in any way liable for any misuse of the information.

Bible references are from the King James Version.

Cover concept and design by Jay Onwukwe. All images used under license from Shutterstock.com

SEXUAL ENERGY TRANSMUTATION

the secret path to
Health, Wealth and Genius

Jay Onwukwe

Also by
Jay Onwukwe

The WEALTH SECRETS
You Must Know Before40

To

Uzoaru Grace Onwukwe

my *amazon* of inestimable value

CONTENTS

SEXUAL ENERGY IS
CREATIVE POTENCY

Sex, the carnal root of Man's *generation*, can be the source of his *degeneration*, yet holds the key to his *regeneration*.

When properly harnessed, the primordial powers of sex and its *creative essences* that initiate all earthly existence can be used to achieve anything you want.

In the *source* of this vital power lie also the sources of Wealth, Health and Genius.

Jay Onwukwe

INTRODUCTION

Through the mechanism of sex, you and I came into this world to experience Life. The same is true for all living creatures on planet earth.

Sex is Nature's primary channel for procreation, preservation and evolution. All living things procreate, multiply and perpetuate their kind through sexual intercourse in one form or another.

As the singular act through which Man expresses his highest creative power of bringing offspring into the world, sexual intercourse is much more than mere conjugal union; it is a profound act of great responsibility, with deep spiritual and mystical connotations.

When couples understand and align with this fact, they have within their reach, the ability to deploy the superlative powers of sex beyond biological procreation of babies - to explore the higher currents of life, and experience the deeper joys and mysteries of human existence on earth.

Indeed, the primordial creative energy in sex transcends procreation. Unfortunately, many men and women being unaware unknowingly dissipate and thus fail to avail themselves of the innate superlative powers of their abundant sex drive; and this is one primary cause of mediocrity.

This book empowers you with basic esoteric knowledge of sex. It presents the secret alchemy of sexual energy transmutation in a simple, practical and natural way, anyone can use. This arcane wisdom, taught only to Kings and Queens and their trusted inner circles in ancient dynasties, is sure to impact your sex life positively.

It is no surprise that *sex* is in constant focus and hype. This is because sexual desire is not only inborn, it is also the strongest desire in Man. Even the baby male child of a few months old sprouts an erection while suckling her mother's breasts, albeit unconsciously.

And because the external sex organs are easily seen and felt, sexual desire is easily aroused. Thus a lot of mental and emotional energies flow into sexual desire and its gratification, even without much conscious effort from us.

When properly indulged in, the sex act produces such exquisite feelings of ecstasy and joy unlike any other; making the desire for physical sexual contact quite intense and irresistible in most men and women.

An *intense desire,* whether for sex, money, politics or sports laurels, is *creative potency* seeking expression or outlet, and you have a choice of how and on what to invest it. The more intense the desire, the stronger the unseen forces propelling its actualisation.

Your thoughts, desires and intentions, and the associated feelings and emotions they generate in you are *creative energies*, differing only in their *colouration* and eventual route of expression or outlet, brought about by the transforming action and power of your Mind - and *sexual desire* is no exception.

In other words, the self-same creative potency projecting as tumultuous sex drive or *sexual energy* can, by a mere switch of intent and focus, become Intellectual energy, Money energy, Professional energy, Political energy, Sports energy, Spiritual energy, or whatever type of energy you need at any point in time.

Sex, the carnal root of Man's *generation*, can be the source of his *degeneration*, yet holds the key to his *regeneration*. When properly harnessed, the primordial powers of sex and its creative essences that initiate all earthly existence can be used to achieve anything you want - for in the source of this vital power lie also the sources of Wealth, Health and Genius. This book tells you how.

This book is intended for adults, especially couples, who desire to enlarge their enjoyment, as well as their knowledge of the mysteries of sex - and thereby derive superior benefits from proper engagement in that profound act of conjugal love.

It aims to stimulate the reader to seek deeper understanding of the mysteries, not just of sex, but of *Life* itself.

CREATIVE ENERGY
The Genesis

Quantum physics reveals that everything, including you and me and the entire universe around us is pure Energy, differing only in rate of vibration. Everything vibrates at its own specific rate, which determines its characteristics.

Similarly, the great scholar, philosopher and scientist, Albert Einstein, stated that energy can neither be created nor destroyed, but merely changes from one form to another.

A physical illustration of this principle is the molecular combination H_2O which can be solid (ice) or liquid (water) or gas (vapour), depending on its rate of vibration at any point in time subject to the prevailing atmospheric conditions of temperature and pressure.

Einstein's energy theory, encapsulated in the universal formula $E=MC^2$, shows that Energy is Matter, and matter is energy. Thus everything is energy.

Further analysis shows that on the lowest vibration or *dense* spectrum is solid matter which can be seen and touched. On the highest vibration or *alpha* spectrum is subtle ether or spirit, which can neither be seen nor touched – such energy vibrations are beyond the sensual perception of humans; but some domestic animals can sense them.

However, even though we do not see and feel it, *spirit essence* enfolds and permeates ALL. In it we live and move and have our being. What the ocean is to the fish, spirit is to Man.

It may help clear any misconceptions and improve our understanding, if we simply say that for the purpose of this discussion,

**THOUGHT IS
CREATIVE ENERGY**

You are today where your Thoughts have brought you; you will be tomorrow where your Thoughts take you.

James Allen

physical refers to things we can see and touch - such as houses, tables, our bodies, etc; while *spiritual* refers to things we can neither see nor touch - such as thought, ideas, emotions, intentions, desires, etc.

Thus, we live in a universe comprised of both the physical and the spiritual worlds. The one, we can see and feel; the other, we can neither see nor feel with our primal senses, yet exists.

The *physical* dominates our awareness because we sense and identify with it all the time. But *spirit* being imperceptible, is virtually ignored, yet everywhere present, potent and operative. Our universe is a countless assortment of potent energy fields of diverse intensities in constant flux.

The *spirit* world begets the *physical* world. The *mental* world begets the *material* world. The *kingdom within* governs the *kingdom without*. Our *inner consciousness* creates our *outer experiences*. The *outside world* mirrors the *inside world*. As in *heaven*, so on *earth*. As *within*, so *without*. As *above*, so *below*. The one is *cause*, the other is *effect*.

God created Man in His own image and likeness. God is Spirit; therefore the real inner Man is spirit. As an essentially spiritual being, Man is under the authority and compulsion of Spirit. Man's primary origin and constituency is Spirituality. When Spirit enthrones and takes full dominion in Man, his *Mind* is at peace, his *Body* is harmonized, and his *Affairs* are ordered.

Just as his creator, whose image and likeness he is, Man is also a creator. Desire stimulates Thought. Man creates through his Thought and Ideas held in Mind. *Thought* is creative Energy; wherever thought goes, energy flows.

> **TO BE ALIVE**
> **IS TO CREATE**
>
> Life is *Consciousness* - the creative awareness of Man. To live is to create - and what you create is up to you.
>
> Jay Onwukwe

Through the law of *mental causation* in action, whatever you passionately desire, you ultimately attract. Thus, any passionate thoughts held in Mind long enough come to fruition. That way, Man creates his *worldly experience* and predicts his *future* outcome.

All men and all women are endowed with abundant *creative energy*. The evolved man or woman is not only aware of this innate potency to create, but has freedom of choice as to its development and deployment for the highest good - a great responsibility.

Man is imbued with the intelligence and wisdom to develop and judiciously use his creative abilities to expand himself and uplift humanity - and this sets him apart from other animals.

Life is *spirit* - the creative essence that animates all Mankind. We can neither see nor touch *Life*, yet it exists. Life, the definitive idea in God-Mind (Genesis 1:26) is invisible, yet reveals itself in birth and death and all activities in-between. Life is activity. To be alive is to be creatively active.

Between the earthly milestones of birth and

death, life is the unbroken flow of creative energy manifestation. Birth and death respectively mark the entry and exit of life. Life is *creative awareness* expressing itself.

Life is the creative potency in Man - to live is to create. Man is constantly exercising this great power - knowingly or unknowingly - through his thoughts, desires and actions.

YOUR MIND IS YOUR INNER KINGDOM

Your Mind is a fertile soil; your Thoughts, Ideas and Desires are seeds; and they yield according to their kind.

Seek first to govern this inner kingdom with *right-thought-ness*, and all other things shall be added unto you.

Jay Onwukwe

Creativity is innate in Man. However, what you create is up to you. Your station in life today is a reflection of how well you have managed your creative ability since birth.

All creativity begins in the invisible - in the crucible of the Mind - as an Idea or Thought which given sufficient *attention*, eventually manifests as things. Therefore seek first to govern this inner kingdom with *right-thought-ness*, and all *outer* things shall be added unto you.

Your Mind is very fertile soil; your *thoughts and desires* are potent seeds, and they yield according to their kind. Thus your Mind, working in accord with *Cosmic Intelligence* brings about your ultimate experience, and indeed your earthly destiny. Surely, you create your world!

**POWERFUL
MOTIVATOR**

Sexual desire is the most powerful of human desires. When driven by this desire, men develop keenness of imagination, courage, will power, persistence, and creative ability unknown to them at other times.

Napoleon Hill

SEX MOTIVE
The Activator

Whenever a man is enthralled by a woman, and he wants her, to have and to hold, a certain state of mind activates in that man. That state of mind is very potent; as it draws out the very best of the man's attributes of keen observation, imagination, courage, tact, persistence and creativity, into a coordinated *battle* plan to capture and possess that very object of his desire, the woman, even if for a fleeting moment.

An intense desire activates mental activity towards its actualization. So strong and compelling is the drive for sexual contact that men risk their prestige, reputation, relationship, business, and even life, just to indulge in it.

When driven by this motive, the mind of man invokes a super-ability for extra-ordinary action. This same state of mind can equally be used to achieve any other goal upon which it is directed – including wealth creation and accumulation.

It is therefore imperative that this natural but tumultuous sex drive must not only be understood, it must also be controlled, reined-in and given balanced and dignified expression through outlets that enrich and uplift the total Man.

This can be achieved through a natural but conscious process of *conservation and transmutation*; if not, sex energy continues to find release through purely physical

> **TAME THE
> SEX BEAST**
>
> Sex alone is a mighty urge to action, but its forces are like a cyclone – they are often uncontrollable....
>
> When the emotion of love begins to mix itself with the emotion of sex, the result is calmness of purpose, poise, accuracy of judgement, and balance.
>
> Napoleon Hill

outlets only, and possibly through other less wholesome vents such as crime and drugs.

Sexual energy transmutation is a conscious re-channelling of this potent creative force, away from purely physical outlets, and into other spheres of endeavour such as arts, intellectual, music, the professions, politics, spirituality, business, sports, etc.

This you can achieve by not always succumbing to seeking physical sexual release each and every time you feel the urge for sex, even if your partner is sitting right there next to you, ready and available. You sometimes need to recognise, revere and salute this *creative potency* surging in you as sexual energy at that very moment, and then re-direct it away from carnal sexual gratification by simply switching your *thoughts* off sex and unto some other very important tasks you need to get done.

The man or woman who expresses a high or excessive sex drive is not favourably looked upon in many societies. However, research reveals that men and women of superior accomplishments throughout history were personalities with highly developed sex natures.

Take a mental survey around you, and you'll find that most successful people are also those with highly developed sex natures. Sexual magnetism or drive, when properly harnessed, is the key to greater personal success.

Sex is a mighty urge to action; but its forces need control and direction. History reveals that for most men of wealth and power, the needed control and guidance came from a harmonious convergence of the desire for

---

**TRUE LOVE
AND ROMANCE**

...Rejoice with the wife of thy youth. Let her be as the loving hind and pleasant roe; let her breasts satisfy thee at all times; and be thou ravished always with her love.

Proverbs 5:18 & 19

sex with the emotion of love and the excitement of romance, usually made possible through the modifying influence of *a loving woman* – be she a wife or mistress.

When a man finally finds his rightful woman, the search ends, as the *butterfly* settles. With the search for true-love over, the scheming and dating that used to consume so much time, effort, mental and emotional energy, all come to an end.

Hence sexual energy begins to conserve and sublimate, as all attention and desire is not only invested, but now converge on the one and only woman in the whole universe that truly matters.

And this is the real root of the modifying influence of a loving woman on a successful man - she is truly his *amazon*, providing just the right admixture of physical, emotional, mental and spiritual solutions that satiate his quest for sex, love and romance - thus inducing *balance* - the perfect state of mind for superior accomplishment.

With such support and modifying influence from the right woman, coupled with an unfolding positive outlook on the future, a man becomes more responsible, focused, self-assured and confident, and therefore more successful.

He becomes truly aware of his foremost responsibility - to work hard to adequately provide for the most important people in his life - the woman and her child. Indeed, *behind every successful man there is a woman.*

Fortunate indeed is the man with a high sex drive, who has also learned the art of sexual energy transmutation. The desire for sexual expression is the strongest and most impelling of all emotions in man. When

---

SEX - A MAJOR SOURCE OF ACTION

Destroy the sex glands, whether in man or beast, and you have removed the major source of action.

Napoleon Hill

---

properly harmonized, the coming together of the desire for sex, with the emotion of love, and the excitement of romance, produces a rare and superior state of mind in Man - a great asset for the attainment of genius and the accomplishment of superior goals.

The mere possession of a high sex drive is not enough for success and genius; it must be effectively controlled and transmuted.

Unfortunately, many men make this destiny changing discovery late in life, if at all; and usually after crossing the peak of their sex drive, which usually occurs before the age of forty-five to fifty.

It stands to reason that for those fortunate enough to know, the same peak period of sex drive can, just by a mere flip of focus and desire, also become the epoch of maximum achievement.

Sexual desire is a major source of action in man. Science reveals that the sex hormones, produced in the internal sex organs, are vital for a properly functioning sexuality. When you destroy the sex glands, whether in man or beast, you removed the major source of action.

For proof, consider what becomes of a castrated man, dog, goat or bull. They grow fat, docile and submissive.

The functions and power of sex was well known to man even in ancient of days. Male servants attending to royal families were, for obvious reasons, usually castrated.

Hills summed up the ultimate consequence of sex alteration thus: *it takes out of the male, whether man or beast, all the fight that was in him.*

**SEXUAL
IMAGINATION**

A woman looks at a woman
to see what she is wearing;

A man looks at a woman
to *see* what she is covering.

Anonymous

There is no drive more powerful than the desire of man for woman. And there is no motive more compelling than man's need to please his woman. Every man wants to appear great in the eyes of the woman – to be a hero. Every man wants to prove to his woman of choice, that he is worth every ounce of her love – to be her *Knight in shining armour.*

When closely scrutinized, all of a man's actions revolve around this desire and this motive. Remove this motive and this drive, and there is nothing to fight for. That is the genesis of the power of women over men.

"No man is happy or complete without the modifying influence of the right woman. The man who does not recognize this important truth deprives himself of the power which has done more to help men achieve success than all other forces combined." Napoleon Hill.

**SEX IS
GOOD**

And God saw everything
that HE had made, and
behold it was very good.

Genesis 1:31

SEXUAL DESIRE
Pro-creative Trigger

Sex is Nature's primary mechanism for procreation, evolution and ge-neration. Sexual desire in man or woman is natural. Therefore, it should not be ignored, suppressed or crushed. It is perfectly normal to have erotic sexual feelings and fantasies, and you should express it, not only responsibly but also respectfully, in ways that enrich the body, stimulate the mind, and uplift the spirit of Man.

In creation, God made man, and made the woman to keep him company; and endowed them with differing, yet mutually attractive physical and sexual attributes that ensure procreation and perpetuity of the human race.

Therefore sex is nothing to be ashamed of, but something to be revered, explored, understood, enjoyed and correctly used for the purpose it was divinely instituted.

Sex is neither dirty nor unholy; in fact, to the contrary, sex is clean and holy, and there should be no misconception about it.

Sexuality is so important in our lives today that a whole range of business activities and industries are propped by it. Marketers, advertisers, designers and many others use both direct and indirect appeal to our sexual desires and emotions to grab our attention in order to achieve their various aims and objectives.

Many multi-million dollar businesses in the fashion, pharmaceutical, beauty, publishing and entertainment sectors - both online and offline - are firmly rooted in sexual desire and its gratification.

**YE ARE
GODS**

The Goddess resides in all women
and the Lord abides in all men.

Jvalavali Vajramala

Unfortunately, inadequate knowledge, plus the undue hype on sexuality lead many to indulge in sexual activities that are not only wasteful, but also self-destructive.

This is aggravated by our over-exposure to, and constant bombardment with unlimited assortment of subtle sexual stimulation and auto-suggestions, which we unconsciously absorb from the print and electronic media, advertisements, films and music, just to mention a few. The result is unending arousal, fantasy and wasteful dissipation of sexual energy - a strand of creative potency.

The desire for sex is not to be condemned or suppressed, but should be understood, appreciated and lifted to its rightful place in the affairs of Man.

With a little thought, it should not be difficult for the discerning mind to see that the same sex-force, which at its primal state produces such intense orgasmic excitement and energy in both men and women can, when transmuted become:

The *fire* in the General's eye;
The *melody* in the Singer's voice;

The *flow* in the Author's pen;
The *warmth* in the Teacher's voice;
The *sprint* in the Athlete's feet;
The *firmness* in a Hand-shake;
The *healing* in the Pastor's hands;
The *radiance* on the Master's face;
The *eloquence* of the Orator;
The *charisma* of the Statesman;
The *genius* of the Professor;
The *charm* of a Lover;
The *acumen* of the Businessman;
The *doggedness* of the Champion;
The *creativity* of the Artist;
The *equanimity* of the Adept;
And so on.

HARMONY

Every time a man wishes to
make love, there is a certain
order of things to be followed.
In the first place, the man
should harmonize his mood
with that of the woman.

Su-Nu-Ching

HARMONIZATION
Water versus Fire

Physical, emotional and spiritual harmonization between couples in sexual union is very necessary if they desire to get maximum benefits from the mutual exchanges that occur at all of these levels. Ideally, the giving and receiving of a gift of sexual intercourse should only be between couples who know, understand, appreciate and truly love each other.

Sexual intercourse should never be a rash and brash affair, or a wait and take thing. Even though there may be physical release, such indulgence is spiritually damaging to one or both partners. A man should carefully harmonize his own enjoyment with that of his partner. When making love, a man should not be selfish or self-centred. He should ensure that the woman thoroughly enjoys herself and reaches her climax of pleasure quickly and frequently.

The surroundings, the context, intimacy and emotional connection are important to the woman. While the man is in a hurry to enter, explore and explode, the woman wants romance and affection - to chat, laugh, kiss and cuddle.

Just as sexual penetration is the emotional trigger for the man, chatting combined with extended foreplay is the emotional trigger for the woman. Just as the man is aroused by what he *sees*, the woman responds more to what she *hears*. While a healthy man needs no preparation for sexual intercourse, it is prolonged foreplay that prepares the woman emotionally and physically for sex. *"Women need a reason to have sex. Men just need a place."* Billy Crystal.

GIVE AND TAKE

A man should learn therefore to touch the woman he loves in such a way that he transmits to her a vivid electric current that trills her with delightful feelings, while it relieves his nervous tensions of accumulated surplus forces.

J. William Lloyd

The man should therefore ensure both physical and emotional harmonization by maintaining firm control over his sensual feelings, as he awaits the woman's slow but steady ascent up the ladder of sexual arousal.

When harmonized couples indulge in sexual intercourse, they generate powerful energy flux that is beneficial to their physical and subtle bodies. Conversely, un-harmonized sexual intercourse produces one-directional energy flow that creates physical, emotional and psychic tension between the partners.

For couples who love and understand each other, the process of harmonization is easily or even unconsciously activated. Observant couples will begin to notice subtle signs from their partner indicating desire for sexual intercourse several hours or even days before consummation. Such subtle signs and body language bring their feelings into harmony, as their desire for physical sexual contact heightens with much expectation towards eventual consummation.

Achieving physical harmony in sexual affairs promotes spiritual harmony; and when the vital life energies are properly harmonized with love and understanding, the result is eternal satisfaction far and above sensual pleasure.

The importance of emotional and spiritual harmony between couples cannot be over-emphasized. Man is fire. Woman is water. If the couples are unselfish, and truly love and respect each other, the heat of the fire will be just hot enough to warm up the water without drying it up; and the cool of the water will be just cool enough to douse the heat without extinguishing the fire. When couples generously give and gratefully, receive sexual pleasures, equilibrium is achieved.

WOMAN IS DELICIOUS

How delicious an instrument is woman when artfully played upon; how capable is she of producing the most exquisite harmonies, of executing the most complicated variations of love, and of giving the most divine of erotic pleasures.

Ananga Ranga

SEXUAL INTERCOURSE
A Mutual Union

As a spiritual being dwelling in a physical world, Man is subject to the laws of spirit, the laws of physics, and the laws of man. Sexual intercourse is an outward ritual of an inner *spiritual* process by which human souls sojourn to mother earth to experience life as we know it.

The joining together of the male and female sex organs in a mutual sexual relationship is an important outward expression of an even more important inward communion of Mind and Spirit. It is thus an act of great spiritual responsibility, with deep mystical connotations. Unfortunately, most couples and sex partners hardly ever consider or even realise these implications.

Sexual intercourse - the joining of the male and female sex organs in mutual union - facilitates the mutual exchange of the male and female essences and secretions. This is especially so, if the point of sexual orgasm and emissions is reached in both partners.

31

Sexual intimacy enables couples in love to explore each other's bodies, touching and feeling each other's most secret places in the most intimate of ways imaginable. By the singular act of willingly and lovingly opening her legs and allowing the man to deeply penetrate her most private and intimate physical space, the woman surrenders herself wholly to the man on all levels of being - physical, emotional and spiritual - making him feel like a conqueror.

**WAIT
FOR HER**

One of man's chief duties is to learn to withhold himself as much as possible and at the same time to hasten the enjoyment of his partner. The desires of the woman are cooler and slower to rouse than those of the man; she is not easily satisfied by a single act of love-making. Her slower excitement demands prolonged embraces and if these are denied her, then she often feels irritated.

Ananga Ranga

When a man and woman who are truly in love enter into harmonious and passionate sexual intercourse, there is nothing in the whole world to surpass the supreme joy of that moment - as an indwelling spring of ecstasy suffuses and envelopes them. This wonderful experience strengthens their physical, emotional and spiritual bonds, and thus makes their relationship stronger and most harmonious. When evolved, sexual intercourse becomes a joyful fellowship of harmonious souls in mutual consent and communion.

Sexual intercourse serves the various needs of Man for recreation, procreation, rejuvenation and spirituality. These are primarily achieved through the fusion of the male and the female sex organs, the sensual feelings it generates, the inter-change of sexual secretions that follow, and the silent conversation of lovers in a sacred communion.

Sexual intercourse has both physical and spiritual components. While the physical component excites with sensual release, and rewards with offspring, the spiritual component bestows heavenly bliss, and rewards with creativity.

Sexual intercourse is much more than erotic seduction and pretentious resistance; much more than male dominance and female robotic submission; much more than being *fucked* or *pounded*; and much more than who *comes* or who does not come. Sexual intercourse should be a relaxed, mutual indulgence of harmonious lovebirds, in physical, emotional and spiritual communion

WOMAN IS
SUPERIOR

Woman is superior to man in the same way that water is superior to fire. People who are expert in the Art of Love are like excellent cooks, who know how to blend the different flavours into a tasty meal. Those who know the Art of Yin and Yang can blend the pleasures of the senses, but those who do not know it will have an unexpected death, without ever having enjoyed love-making.

Tantric Wisdom

that ultimately leads to blissful ecstasy and physical rejuvenation for both partners.

For optimum benefits, wise couples should know for what particular purpose they indulge in sexual intercourse; they must strive to raise their sexual union from the level of thoughtless carnal indulgence and unto the superior level of a mutually bonding communion.

As couples grow older together in love, understanding and mutual respect for each other, their relationship grows stronger and harmonious. It then becomes easier for them to raise their sexual union above the carnal level and unto the glorious heights.

When such couples enter into sexual intercourse in mutual desire, love and affection for each other, they are bound to ascend unto and remain on that ecstatic height of joy and satisfaction that subsists even after all the sensations of physical orgasm have long receded.

As the singular act through which Man expresses his highest creative power of bringing an offspring unto earth, sexual intercourse is much more than physical conjugation. It is a personal act of great responsibility that carries deep spiritual and mystical connotations.

When couples understand this, they have within their reach, the ability to deploy the superlative powers of sex beyond biological procreation - to explore the deeper joys and blessings of life.

MUCH MORE THAN PHYSICAL CONJUGATION

As the singular act through which Man expresses his highest creative power of bringing new souls unto earth, sexual intercourse is much more than physical conjugation. It is an act of great responsibility, with deep spiritual and mystical connotations.

Jay Onwukwe

MUTUAL EXCHANGE
The Equalizer

The ultimate consequence of couples giving or accepting a gift of sexual intercourse is the mutual exchange of life essences between them at the physical as well as spiritual levels.

During sexual intercourse, the male and female sex organs are physically joined in mutual union. This facilitates the mutual exchange of the male and female essences, body fluids and secretions, especially if the point of physical climax and emissions is reached in both partners.

Such mutual absorption is beneficial to both partners, and conscious effort should be made to indulge in it. The man absorbs through the head of the penis, while the woman absorbs through the walls of the vagina and the womb. Mutual absorption is enhanced if the penis is left in the vagina for as long as possible without ejaculation.

However, while mutual exchanges take place on the physical level through the mixing and absorption of sexual secretions and body fluids, spiritual exchanges also take place on the psychic and karmic levels. While the physical exchanges are obvious, the psychic and karmic exchanges may be imperceptible to one or both partners, depending on the depth of their knowledge of sexual secrets.

BEWARE OF STRANGERS

And why wilt thou, my son, be ravished with a strange woman, and embrace the bosom of a stranger?

Her house is the way to hell, going to the chambers of death.

Proverbs 5:20, 7:27

For a harmonized and balanced couple, these mutual exchanges are beneficial, healthy and desirable, because they enhance their subtle bodies and strengthen their relationship. But for the inharmonious or strange bed fellows, who may be spiritually and psychically mismatched, such exchanges are sure to harm at least one of the partners.

Therefore a gift of sexual intercourse should not be carelessly given or accepted, because it carries within it hidden consequences than what is physically felt by the partners.

This very fact points to how and why an older man or woman, a sugar daddy or sugar mummy, who is knowledgeable about sexual secrets, can take advantage of younger lovers to cleanse his or her spiritual body, as well as rejuvenate his or her physical body.

IMMORTALITY

Heaven is lasting
and Earth enduring.
The reason for this
is that they do not
live for themselves
alone; therefore
they live long.

Tao Te Ching

SPIRITUAL COMMUNION
Two are One

The outward physical expression of love through sexual intercourse presents a great opportunity to couples for self-discovery. However, to attain higher vistas of self expression, a couple should do much more than explore each other's physical bodies. They must also strive to harmonize their emotional, psychic and spiritual bodies.

For the truly harmonious couple, sexual intercourse when properly entered into is much more than physical communion; it is also a spiritual re-union. The feeling of oneness that envelops the couple during and after copulation is a truly mystical experience that opens the door to spiritual transcendence. When couples engage in regular harmonious physical intercourse, spiritual bonding is strengthened.

Therefore, the wise couple should strive to raise their acts of sexual union from the common level of mere physical intercourse, unto the higher levels of sensitive love-making. And when the flames of sexual passion are properly blended, they can purify and transform sensual desire into spiritual ecstasy.

PROTECT YOURSELF

In love-making, the semen must be regarded as a most precious substance; by saving it, a man protects his life.

Taoist Wisdom

SEMEN
Most Precious Possession

Science reveals that healthy semen contains vital nutrients, trace elements, amino acids, and vitamins in purified form, as well as one half of the cells required for procreation.

Taoism teaches that semen is a man's most precious possession. It is not to be wasted because it is the living essence, containing all the physical and spiritual attributes of the man.

Furthermore, there is a psycho-physical link between a man and his sperm long after ejaculation. Sperm is the procreative cell in the semen that fertilizes the female egg for conception to take place.

Outside the body, ejaculated sperm can survive for quite a while; as such, ejaculated sperm should be treated with respect, and must not be allowed into the hands of unscrupulous people who can misuse its potency.

Many youths unknowingly waste this most precious substance through riotous living fuelled by their greed for the female body and beauty, and their insatiable quest for sensual gratification. This propels them to focus and invest so much time and creative energy on the female body and how to bring about physical sexual contact with it. If not checked, such habits inevitably result in loss of focus, mediocrity and a wasted youth life.

Semen is man's most precious possession. As such, male masturbation that habitually culminates in emission of semen is like a thief in his own house, stealing his own precious gems.

PRIMORDIAL SOURCE

One should not eject this *camphor* casually. It is from this substance that the Yoginis have their origin. Its nature is that of Supreme Joy. It is indestructible and luscious, as pervasive as the sky.

Hevajra Tantra

SUPPRESSION
A losing Battle

Suppression of sexual desire is un-natural; it is a battle you cannot win because you swim against a powerful natural current. Suppressed sexual desire is like an active volcano waiting to erupt; a disaster that is bound to happen at a most awkward moment, causing embarrassment and disgrace.

Prolonged suppression of sexual energy can result into restlessness and loss of concentration. That is why the neophyte is always admonished not to bottle-up sexual energy, but to find suitable release, so that he can regain concentration and be able to focus on the work at hand.

Excessive sexual energy need not be suppressed; it should rather be harnessed and channelled into other areas of creativity in arts, music, sports, literature, academics, business, politics, the professions, etc.

Rather than suppress it, sexual desire should be blissfully satiated in a harmonious and dignified way, such that frequent depletion of life essence is minimized.

Suppression of sexual desire is not the same as transmutation of sexual energy. While suppression may be painful and difficult, transmutation is pleasurable and effortless.

To occasionally deny oneself the wonderful sensations of a purely physical orgasm, is a price worth paying for the more enduring prize of good health, magnetism, intuition and mental acumen. Every *prize* has its *price*.

ABSTINENCE IGNITES
THE SPIRITUAL FLAME

Great spiritual Masters
went apart awhile, up the hill,
unto the mountains or into
the wilderness, before
embarking on great spiritual
missions that left indelible
marks on Humanity.

ABSTINENCE
Stokes the Fire

bstinence or sexual fast is the avoidance of sexual intercourse for a short while. Controlled abstinence from sex is a potent routine that is quite beneficial to the whole body system – physical, mental, emotional and spiritual.

For optimum benefit and effectiveness, periodic fasting should not be about food and water alone, it must be a holistic programme that includes fasting from sex, keeping the body temple holy and purging oneself of negative emotions, thoughts, words and actions, not just during the period only, but even after.

Fasting from food and sex stokes the spiritual flame in man and helps to purge his negative emotions. Spiritual masters recognize the need to routinely abstain from sex; and when rightly practiced, this helps to boost their spiritual potency and efficacy.

Periodic abstinence, coupled with fasting and prayer for seven, fourteen, or twenty-one days can stimulate, strengthen and boost spirituality.

Great spiritual Masters went apart awhile, up the hill, into the mountains or into the wilderness for much longer periods, before embarking on great spiritual missions that left indelible marks on Humanity.

Going apart awhile, into the hills or unto the mountains, all connote the same thing - aloneness, meditation, fasting and praying. When correctly executed, fasting from food and sex can activate magical powers, or even spiritual illumination in Man.

EUNUCHS

For there are eunuchs that were so born from their mother's womb; and there are eunuchs that were made eunuchs of men; and there are eunuchs which have made themselves eunuchs for the kingdom of heaven's sake.

Jesus (Matthew 19:12)

Sexual abstinence is an effective way to accumulate and concentrate vital life-force and essences within the body. During abstinence, sexual energy is conserved, and the accumulated life-force and essences re-circulate within the body, nourishing and stimulating the power centres.

When you observe a period of sexual abstinence, the quantum and potency of semen, as well as the immune system is boosted; and this can be of immense benefit to those suffering from such ailments as impotency and low sperm count.

Indeed, with proper guidance, a barren woman can conceive after observing a specific period of abstinence from sexual intercourse. Similarly, impotent men can be helped to regain potency and successfully impregnate their wives, through a regime of treatment that includes strictly observed periods of controlled abstinence.

Sexual abstinence is beneficial to the brain. And with a well nourished brain you have greater capacity for higher levels of mental activity: logic, acumen, perception, insight, intuition and creative imagination - the very essentials for personal success and superior accomplishments. The practice of creative meditation during periods of sexual fast is quite effective.

Remember, abstinence is only a means to an end, not the end itself. Therefore, except for special purposes, prolonged abstinence from sex is not advisable; this can cause destructive sexual currents to build up within the body. As in most activities in life, the point of diminishing return must be avoided. Balance is Nature's way.

THE SECRET OF VITALITY

If a man knows how to make love without emitting semen, then his vital essence will return within. This is the secret of life, which greatly benefits the system.

Su-Nu-Ching

CONTINENCE
The Accumulator

Continence is the retention of semen within the body through avoidance of ejaculation during sexual contact. During sexual intercourse, the man has two options. He may gradually climb the ladder of sexual excitement to reach its peak and point of no return that culminates in orgasmic ejaculation.

This is the procreative union in which the man chooses to exceed the limits of voluntary control and tumble into the irreversible stages that produce a physical climax and the emission of semen.

Or he may choose to exert some measure of control, such that he thoroughly enjoys himself and satisfies his partner; tethering often on the brink of ecstasy but never succumbing to the ever surging urge to explode into orgasm.

This is the social union in which the man tactfully remains within the zone of voluntary self control, effectively holding back a physical climax, and thus avoids the emission of semen.

In the former, the vital life-forces flow downwards and out of the body via the phallus, to achieve procreation or to waste. But in the later, vital life-forces are retained and re-directed upwards through the spinal column to nourish, not only the brain cells, but also the major energy centres of the body.

**VITALITY
AND GENIUS**

Master Jung was an adept
at nurturing and controlling
his physical functions. He
absorbed new essences from
the Mysterious Valley of woman.
The main point of this art is to
prevent one's potency from dying.
The "returned semen" strengthens
the vitality and nourishes the brain.

Lieh-Hsien-Chuan

Continence is the retention of semen within the body by avoiding ejaculation during sexual intercourse. For this to happen, the usual unconscious surge towards a climax, orgasm and ejaculation must be consciously controlled.

During sexual intercourse, you can choose to maintain absolute control by being fully conscious of the progressively rising current of sexual excitement in your body. This empowers you to know just when to pull the brakes and avoid a voluptuous rapture that leads to emission of semen.

For the man not versed in sexual secrets, his major purpose for every act of sexual intercourse is to experience a rapturous ejaculation and the wonderful sensations it brings. Similarly, a woman derives a subtle sense of satisfaction and accomplishment if she makes her man to offload his semen with an eruptive orgasm that leaves him completely but delightfully devastated.

However, tantric wisdom cautions everyman to regulate the emission of semen according to his store of vital essence. He should never force himself to ejaculate.

A man should not be greedy for female beauty and body. There is no wisdom in allowing every act of sexual intercourse to end in ejaculation of semen, which often leads to physical collapse thereafter. This is damaging to both the body and the psyche.

Also the intuitive and intelligent woman should be able to discern and meet her lover's needs, while satisfying her own desires as well. She needs not demand an ejaculation or extract one from him, even when he obviously does not want to.

SOURCE OF POWER

If one moves but does not emit semen, the life force and vigour are in excess. The body absorbs the energy and all the senses are sharpened.

Peng Tsu

To help retain his semen during sexual intercourse, the man should always indulge in prolonged foreplay with his partner, so that she can reach her orgasm quickly and frequently. That way, she is satisfied, and he is then at liberty to conserve his essence.

Retention of semen through the avoidance of frequent ejaculation is the key to power, vitality and virility.

SUBLIMATION

Through conservation,
sexual energy accumulates
and sublimates into its higher
and more magnificent nature.

CONSERVATION
The Preserver

Sexual energy conservation can be achieved through abstinence and continence. Observing periodic abstinence from sex conserves your vital essence, and this helps to boosts your spiritual, mental and creative energies.

Conserved life essence makes you look younger, healthier and charismatic; you stand out in any crowd due to increased personal magnetism. On the contrary, depletion makes you feel exhausted and irritable; as you look deflated and ordinary.

Through the practice of abstinence and continence, sexual energy sublimates and re-circulates within your body, nourishing your power centres, including the brain cells. This helps to strengthen your spiritual aura, revitalize your internal body functions and energize your physical body.

You grow in confidence and charisma, and you become more attractive to the opposite sex. Through conservation, sexual energy accumulates and sublimates into its higher and more magnificent nature.

Couples who enjoy sex energy conservation by indulging in bonding sexual union live above the psychological burden of satisfying or ministering unto each other's animalistic desires. Their union is elevated from the mundane to the esoteric, as their once separate sexual fantasies converge into one harmonious trip into transcendental ecstasy. Such couples become spiritually harmonized and physically rejuvenated.

DEPLETION VERSUS CONSERVATION

Conservation keeps you
young, healthy and magnetic.
Depletion makes you
feel and look deflated,
weak and ordinary.

In addition to its health and spiritual benefits, the practice of sexual energy conservation goes a long way to help avoid unwanted maternity or paternity, because the risk of conception without intention is to a large extent eliminated.

Other benefits include improved vitality, vigour and personal magnetism, improved powers of imagination, keen observation, clarity of thought, intuition and insight.

Through conservation, the vital essences contained in the sexual fluids are retained and re-distributed within the body, to strengthen the total being, and bestow long-term benefits on man. Therefore, instead of wasting vital life-force through frequent sexual release, you rather conserve it, to naturally nourish your body, sustain your virility, and stimulate your brain cells.

Ideally, a man should consolidate his practice of sexual energy conservation as soon as he is done with procreation.

**SEAT OF
POWER**

The sex organs are the
repository of man's utmost
creative energy – the power
to bring new life unto earth.

THE SEX ORGANS
Tree of Life and Death

In the male, the penis and testes are the primary sex organs. The testes produce the hormone Testosterone as well as Sperm. Testosterone is the hormone that induces important secondary male sexual characteristics such as facial hairs, the thin waist and broad shoulders shape, and broad vocal cords.

The sperm from the male contains one-half of the creative essence required to form new life or offspring.

In the female, the vagina and ovaries are primary sex organs. The ovaries produce Oestrogen and Eggs. Oestrogen is the hormone that induces secondary female sexual characteristics such as development or enlargement of the breasts and widening of the pelvis, growth of pubic hairs and deposition of body fat in hips and thighs.

The Egg from the female contains one-half of the creative essence required to the form new life or offspring. A successful coming together of the two halves - one from the male and one from the female - marks the beginning of new life.

The sex organs are therefore the natural repository of man's most powerful creative energy – the power to bring forth new life or creation. And *"In the source of this vital power lie the sources of endless wealth."* Napoleon Hill.

CUPS OF PLENTY

Energy centres are your cups of plenty which must be held upright to fill to overflowing.

ENERGY CENTRES
Cups of Plenty

The primary energy centres in the body are the Perineum or Root, the Sacral, the Solar Plexus, the Heart, the Thorax, between the Eye Brows, and top of the Head.

Energy centres or chakras are not just the physical locations within or on the body as their names suggest, but etheric counterparts of the related organs or parts of the body. They are channels for energy interface and flow between the various levels of our being. They function as hubs for energy interaction and distribution between our finer and denser vibrations, between our inner and outer worlds, and between our spiritual and physical bodies.

Each energy centre relates to and governs a particular faculty or aspect of your life or being. It is your primary duty to develop and activate these *cups of plenty*. That way you keep your channels open for more blessings to flow in. The seven major energy centres and their areas of dominance and

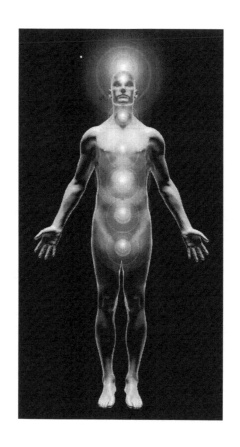

THE SEVEN MAJOR
ENERGY CENTRES

influence are briefly explored below.

The *Root*, located at the base of the spine, in the vicinity of the reproductive organs, is the energy centre for pro-creativity, self-identity, and self-worth or self-esteem. It governs your career choice or path, as well as your wealth mindset.

The quality associated with this centre is *Sensation*; its colour is Red. It manifests as your level of control over matters of Sex, and other lower vibration thought forms such as Fear, Anger, Jealousy, Revenge, Greed and Selfishness.

When balanced and active, you experience good health, high self-esteem, emotional harmony, and poise.

The *Sacral*, closely associated with the Root and located just above it in the region of the lower abdomen, is the energy centre for sexuality, relationship, and creativity. The faculty associated with this centre is the *Personality*; its colour is Orange. It governs the quality and calibre of your Desires, Ambitions and Aspirations.

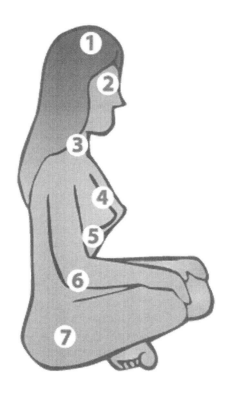

THE SEVEN MAJOR
ENERGY CENTRES

1 - Crown   2 - Forehead

3 - Thorax   4 - Heart

5 - Plexus   6 - Sacral

7 - Root

When active and balanced, there is a strong and focused personality, productivity, and well-rounded success in all spheres of life.

The *Solar Plexus*, located just above the navel, is the energy centre that governs such qualities as discernment, instinct, learning and wisdom. The power associated with this centre is the *Intellect*; its colour is Yellow. It manifests as the ability for clear thinking, logic and reasoning.

A well developed and active solar plexus is discernible as a high level of self confidence, personal magnetism and inner power.

The *Heart* is the energy centre for the emotions: love, compassion and sympathy. The attributes associated with this centre is Security and Relationship; its colour is Green. It governs your self-acceptance and emotional stability – your capacity to freely give and receive love, sympathy, tolerance and forgiveness.

An evolved and active Heart centre comes across as that personality capable of strong feelings, great acts of self-sacrifice and deep compassion.

The *Thorax* is the energy centre for vocal expression and communication of your thoughts, ideas and emotions. The ability or power associated with this energy centre is *Communication*; its colour is Blue. It reveals your inner qualities through your *true voice* – eloquent, rich, warm, mellow, soothing, persuasive or commanding.

When developed, there is uniqueness of vocal sound, power of oration, and clear diction.

THE CROWN

The *Crown*, located at the top of the head, is the energy centre for detachment, purification and sublimation. When active, there is spiritual fulfilment, balance and eternal joy.

The *Centre of Forehead* (in-between the eye brows), often referred to as the third eye, is the energy centre for spiritual perception, illumination and detachment. The power associated with this centre is *Intuition*; its colour is Indigo. It manifests as *Inner Guidance* – the power to *know,* without knowing why or how.

When activated, it sharpens your intuition, imagination and perception; creating inner beauty, equanimity, empathy and charisma.

The *Crown*, located at the top of the head, is the energy centre for balance, surrender, purification and sublimation. The power associated with this centre is *Imagination*; its colour is Violet. Its attribute is *Divine Consciousness* - man's ardent quest for his divinity; the innate desire to re-connect to his divine source - GOD. When activated, there is spiritual fulfilment and eternal joy.

Energy centres are your *cups of plenty*, which must be activated and nurtured, to function optimally and become filled to overflowing, to bless you and all of mankind.

CREATIVE
GENIUS

Sex energy is the creative energy
of all geniuses. There never has
been, and never will be a great
leader, builder, or artist lacking
in this driving force of sex.

The energy must be transmuted
from desire for physical contact
into some other form of desire
and action before it will lift one
to the status of a genius.

Napoleon Hill

TRANSMUTATION
The Liberator

To transmute is to change in nature or form; alter in essence (*Webster*). In alchemy, transmutation is the supposed change of a *baser* metal into another of *greater* value. Ancient alchemists reputedly tried to transmute Lead into Gold through secret chemical processes in their hideouts.

But for Man and his *thoughts*, *Mind* is the crucible in which the alchemy of energy transmutation takes place. It is in the Mind of man that one type of thought *energy* or desire transmutes into another. Through conscious Mind action - *focus and intent* - man can restructure and project mental energy forms to yield forth their physical equivalents.

Sexual energy naturally builds-up in the body of a healthy man or woman who refrains from excessive or wasteful sexual activities; and who indulges in the sex act with love and harmony. Such accumulated sexual energy gradually converts into other energy forms, which the man or woman can draw upon at times of need.

In its primal form, sexual energy is stored in the Root or Sex Chakra at the base of the spine; but when conserved, it accumulates, sublimates and moves up through the spinal cord, into the other energy centres of the body, especially the *Crown*.

This natural sublimation process takes place even without any conscious effort by you; and you could actually transmute sexual energy without knowing it. However, being knowledgeable and aware of this raw but potent creative energy available to you, and

CONSCIOUS ACTIVATION

While a naturally induced process of sublimation slowly re-directs accumulated sexual energy into other creative outlets, *Transmutation* is a focused conscious activation of the sublimation process.

directing it purposefully, greatly amplifies its effectiveness and its potential to yield superior outcomes.

While a naturally induced normal process of sublimation slowly re-directs sexual energy into other creative outlets, *transmutation* is a conscious activation of the sublimation process.

Sexual energy transmutation re-channels sexual potency into genius and creativity. It is a conscious switch of the urge for physical sensual release, into a surge of mental and emotional stimuli.

Transmutation re-channels the ever surging creative energies in man, away from a wasteful downward and outward flow, into a beneficial inward and upward return that nourishes and invigorates the body and the brain.

Accumulated sexual energy sublimates into superior creative abilities which manifest in various forms depending on your personal needs, aspirations, disposition, pursuits and capabilities.

Thus, based on your peculiar circumstances, you may experience stronger intuition, increased mental alertness, improved clarity of thought, greater understanding of issues, persistence, faith, courage and enthusiasm that propel you to higher pedestals of success in your endeavour or niche.

Sublimation creates a natural reservoir of creative energy which when harnessed and properly directed manifests as greater vistas of Love, Faith, Imagination, Intuition, Order, Judgement and Understanding; plus the Will and the Zeal to take requisite actions that make your aspirations and intentions come to fruition.

THE SECRET OF GREAT ACHIEVERS

The men of greatest achievement are men with highly developed sex natures, men who have learned the art of sex transmutation.

Napoleon Hill

Sublimated sexual energy, as pure creative potency, is a great reservoir of all shades of spiritual, emotional, mental and physical powers, which man can draw upon in times of need for:

—- Acts of great courage and bravery
—- Scientific research and breakthrough
—- Scholastic and intellectual works
—- Great works of art and music
—- Oratory and statesmanship
—- Spiritual revelations and breakthrough
—- Leadership and personal success
—- Wealth creation and accumulation
—- Excellence in competitive sports.
—- And much more.

Thought is an invisible creative energy that is always on duty. Wherever thought goes energy flows. Thus, after the *butterfly* years, as Man matures in mind and body, and as the fires of youth naturally begin to subside, less attention or creative energy is invested on matters of sex. This frees up mental, emotional and spiritual energies to flow into other important issues of life. This is the natural onset of sexual energy sublimation, albeit unconsciously.

The young man or woman who a few years back, could not resist an invitation to an all night party, but who now prefers to sit back at home to prepare a business plan for a new project, write a few more pages of a new book, or prepare for an upcoming professional test, is even without conscious effort already transmuting sexual energy: an opportunity for physical sexual contact is traded for an opportunity to attain higher goals in life; the urge for sensual excitement is turned into a surge of mental activity.

**TRANSMUTATION
IS THE KEY**

The desire for sexual expression is by far the strongest and most impelling of all the human emotions, and for this very reason this desire, when harnessed and transmuted into action other than that of physical expression, may raise one to great accomplishment.

Napoleon Hill

The beneficial effects of sexual energy conservation on the mind and body are not in doubt. Great mentors, coaches and sports administrators know this; and they take necessary steps to protect their protégée or team members from dissipating vital life-force just before important competitions. That way, pent-up sexual energy is allowed to conserve and transmute into alertness, doggedness, dexterity, speed, focus and a passionate craving for laurels.

In whatever field of activity or endeavour, when you successfully convert the pent-up craving for physical sexual expression into a strong passionate surge for victory and laurels, you have a winning formula. One of the greatest and most charismatic boxers of all times, Mohamed Ali was reputed to have known and effectively applied this wisdom to stylishly demolish many of his equally great opponents.

For couples who enjoy mutual respect and harmonious relationship, any premeditated sexual communion activates the flow of creative energy currents in both partners. Such energy flows can be directed towards procreation; or invested on the enjoyment of a purely physical sexual release; or it could be transmuted into mental and emotional stimuli for the accomplishment of superior goals.

Although yogic techniques and creative meditation exercises are reputed to activate the process of sexual energy transmutation in the individual, the practice of sexual energy transmutation by couples completing and balancing each other through the enjoyment of successive peaks of rapture during sexual intercourse is easy, natural, effective and appropriate for harmonized couples.

A WINNING FORMULA

In whatever field of activity, when you transmute the pent-up craving for sexual release into a strong and passionate surge for victory and laurels, you have a winning formula.

The practice of sexual energy transmutation requires that couples engage themselves in very gentle and affectionate intercourse that does not always end in physical climax for any of the partners. By gently moving but never crossing the point of no return, *desire is satiated without energy dissipated*. Such bonding indulgence keeps the body system charged and full of energy, which can then be channelled into other useful activities.

Couples desirous of transmuting sexual energy should always enter into the sex act with over-flowing love and affection for each other. Since health, mental and spiritual benefits, not physical orgasm or ejaculation are the primary objectives, movement if at all should be very slow and gentle. Positions that do not allow for much movement, but which allow deep penetration, caressing, cuddling and fondling should be adopted.

Success in this desirable act requires the willpower and self discipline to control the ever rising tide of sexual excitement in the body. The urge to exceed the limits of physical control and explode into orgasm can be overcome by keeping in focus the primary purpose of the engagement, as well as its superior benefits. Couples should as much as possible, resist the trade-off.

If during any such engagements the couples approach the height of sexual excitement, they should cease all motion, breathing deeply and slowly. This is to avoid crossing the point of no return that culminates in orgasm and emission of semen. The woman's cooperation is critical at this point, as any further movement by her could trigger a physical orgasm for one or both partners, which effectively ends the session, albeit unintentionally.

ACTIVATE THE GENIE IN YOU

Upward re-channelling of sexual energy opens the door into the *Super-Mind*, through which man may know all there is to know about anything he focuses his Thoughts upon.

By approaching the verge, yet avoiding a physical climax, the couples tether on the brink of pleasurable ecstasy, while mentally absorbing, circulating and re-channelling sexual energy upwards - as they explore this euphoric summit together - and this can go on for as long as they desire.

As their physical sensations and breathing gradually subside, they cling to each other, deeply connected, calm and peaceful in complete unity of mind, body and soul. In this transcendental mood, TWO are ONE, in a pure spiritual union that heals ALL - mind, body and affairs.

The couple should remain in this sublime mood for as long as possible. This allows the creative essences to fully reverse their downward movement and return upwards to nourish the energy centres and brain cells, inducing vitality and mental alertness.

This upward re-channelling of sexual energy helps open the door into the *Super-Mind*, through which man may know all there is to know about anything he directs his thoughts upon.

With sensual passion temporarily reined-in, the Mind is now serene and receptive, ready to unravel any problems thrust upon it; and with the self-same magnitude and intensity of creativity, imagination and focus that the sex urge activates in man.

The key to success in energy transmutation is the rechanneling of that *creative potency* now projecting as *sexual desire*, away from animalistic carnal indulgence, and into more sublime mental and spiritual expressions or outlets that are very dear to your heart. This surge of creative ability must be re-directed and invested in a more important alternative outlet or desire you are passionate about.

YOU CAN CRACK THE CODE

The whole idea is to switch focus away from sex, and into cracking the code, but with the self-same intensity of craving that the sex-urge whips up in you.

Therefore while in this calm and relaxed mood, the couple should individually focus on the future they desire and the goals they set to achieve; firmly engraving such clear mental images upon their minds.

Self development activities such as sitting for ideas, meditation, affirmations, creative visualization, mind programming, master mind alliance, can be very effective in the hours and days following.

The hours and days following are just right for creative imagination and visualization exercises: filling your mind with Love, Peace and Harmony; affirming success, health and prosperity; setting superior goals in Mind; seeing clear mental images of the future You; silently or audibly decreeing whatever you want and taking possession of it in your mind. Remember, it all begins in your Mind! *If you can see it in your head, you can hold it in your hands.*

The whole idea is to switch focus away from sex, and into *cracking the code*, but with the self-same intensity of craving that the sex-urge whips up in you. This you can achieve by assuaging the fires of sexual desire, but without dissipating the potency back of it, by not succumbing to the eruptive orgasms that deflate and deplete your emotional, mental, spiritual and physical energies.

Transmutation is akin to *taming the beast*, in which raw tumultuous sexual desire is never suppressed, but effectively reined-in, re-focused and re-deployed to some other productive work.

With sexual desire satiated, but its creative potency not dissipated, you are at liberty to transmute this power into any other type of power you want: *money power, intellectual power, sports power, professional power, spiritual power, political power,* etc, and

---

**REIN-IN AND REDEPLOY
THE SEXUAL BEAST**

Transmutation is akin to *taming the beast*, by which tumultuous sexual desire is effectively reined-in, refocused and redeployed to other productive outlets.

---

deploy it with the same intensity of focus, zeal and will power already activated in you.

Empowered with greater presence of mind, high energy levels, enthusiasm and vitality, you have all it takes to function better and achieve more in all sphere of your life.

Indeed, all you need do is leverage on your newly acquired *alpha resonance* status to create whatever you want. With mental and emotional energies optimized, you are now open and receptive to inspiration from on-high. Miraculously, people and opportunities begin to appear from *nowhere* to advance your pursuits. Talk of serendipity!

With your mind and body now resonating at alpha frequencies, you can *order* whatever you want from the universe and have it delivered to your doorstep.

Thought is masculine; *emotion* is feminine energy. You must align your thought with your emotion to create your reality. Your thought must impregnate your emotion for it to birth-forth your desire or intent. The high energy levels activated in you through *satiation without dissipation* is necessary for success in all form of creativity, including wealth creation and accumulation.

In other words, when through creative imagination you rouse and feel the same emotions you will feel if your desires were already fulfilled, you automatically send a powerful *command* to your subconscious mind to bring it about; and then *universal intelligence* takes over to attract and reveal to you all the resources required to make your mental imagery a physical reality.

By purposefully re-directing your attention away from physical sexual gratification, and into the realization of some higher desirable

---

**SUBLIMATION
IS NATURAL**

Sexual energy naturally builds-up in the body of any healthy man or woman who refrains from excessive or wasteful sexual activity; and who indulges in the sex act with love and harmony.

objectives, but with the self-same intensity of emotional energy and mental dexterity usually generated by the quest for sex, you activate and avail yourself of the superior attributes required to achieve whatever you want. That is sexual energy transmutation.

In his all-time classic, *Think And Grow Rich*, Napoleon Hill describes sexual desire thus:

As the most compelling of all desires in man, the sex urge when effectively harnessed and channelled towards worthwhile goals, its inherent power to bring out the very best of a man's imagination, keen observation, courage, alertness and persistence, remains intact. These attributes, when fully developed and utilized, can raise one man above the other.

For optimum pleasure and success, couples entering into sexual intercourse for the purpose of energy transmutation must ensure that conditions and settings are right and conducive. Most importantly, there must be emotional and spiritual harmony, love and mutual respect between the couples.

Intercourse positions that put undue stress on one or both partners, or any parts of their bodies should be avoided. Couples should experiment to discover what suits them best.

The beddings, the room and surroundings should be orderly and beautiful; and the environment peaceful and serene, devoid of noise and distractions. Privacy must be assured. There must be no intrusion or fear of such during the exercise.

While couples may indulge in this exercise as often as they desire, the need for balance in all human activities, including sex, must be emphasized. The exquisite pleasures and sensations of a *bar-none* voluptuous sexual gratification is not only desirable, but quite

> **A WOMAN IN LOVE**
> **IS A PARTNER**
> **IN PROGRESS**
>
> With the self-same power
> of sex, a woman can uplift
> or bring down a man.

necessary for a wholesome and balanced personality, and should be indulged in. However, the mental and spiritual benefits of sexual intercourse must be emphasized over and above the fleeting sensations of the flesh. As always, balance is the key.

Indeed, even without much effort, but by simply being in the *know* and in the *flow*, anyone can effectively transmute sexual energy. Through self control and proper engagement in sexual activities, sexual energy is conserved. As the conserved vital essence sublimates and re-circulates within your body, it nourishes and strengthens your energy centres, increasing your brain power and intuition. All you need is to be conscious of, and creatively deploy these potent powers available to you, and you're sure to achieve great results.

Anyone aiming for true greatness and success in life must combine the wisdom of energy transmutation with the self-discipline of spirituality. Indeed, power without control is dangerous. To successfully accumulate potent energy only to waste it on negative emotions such as anger, envy, revenge or hatred; or fritter it away due to lack of self-control over the desires of the flesh, is a great loss indeed.

Therefore the hours and days following must be lived purposefully, in positive expectation and with undivided attention fixed on your *dreams and visions*. You must have some other equally strong and passionate desire into which this transmuted energy flows.

BENEFITS OF
SEX ENERGY
TRANSMUTATION

Vitality and Vigour
Personal Magnetism
Mental Sagacity and Acumen
Power of keen Observation
Power of Concentration
Intuition or Sixth Sense
Immunity and Potency
Sexual Attractiveness
Self Confidence
High Self-esteem
Spiritual Evolution

Strive to remain at your best, eating moderately, and exercising regularly. Avoid toxic drinks such as alcohol that diminish brain power. Regular practice of meditation is beneficial. Beware of energy leaks that can occur through quarrels and arguments.

One primary benefit of sexual energy transmutation is increased brain power. With a tremendous brain power comes deeper perception, sharper intuition, greater zeal and dogged determination – the very basic constituents of success in any endeavour.

And with a little spiritual effort in *meditation and silence*, you can acquire the ability to freely and regularly commune with *Infinite Intelligence*, and gain unfettered access into the inexhaustible storehouse of great *Ideas* - the secret genesis of creativity and genius.

Watch your Mind! Learn to regularly become still and aware of the constant stream of rich ideas flowing through your Mind. Success and prosperity are sure to become your normal life experience when you habitually take inspired actions based on the ideas and inspirations revealed to you in the *Silence*.

Men of fame and fortune develop the rare ability to regularly and quietly *tune-in* to the *Cosmic Intelligence* frequency, receive great *Ideas* and inspiration, and act upon them promptly, in a logical sequence that yields great results.

Other benefits of sex energy transmutation include:

Improved vitality and vigour
Improved mental sagacity and acumen
Increased personal magnetism
Improved powers of keen observation

> ### TRANSMUTATION
> ### IS THE KEY
>
> Sex, the carnal root of Man's *generation*, can be the source of his *degeneration*, yet holds the key to his *regeneration*. When properly harnessed, the primordial powers of sex and its *creative essences* that initiate all earthly existence can be used to achieve anything you want.

Improved powers of concentration
Improved Intuition or sixth sense
Improved immunity, potency and virility
Increased attractiveness to the opposite sex
Improved self confidence and self-control
Improved conscious awareness
Improved self-esteem or self-worth
Accelerated spiritual evolution

Lucky is the man blessed with a sex partner who understands, enjoys and lovingly collaborates with him in the practice of sexual energy conservation, circulation and transmutation.

A woman in love is a partner in progress. It is therefore the man's duty to gently teach and lovingly encourage his partner to evolve with him. With the self-same power of sex, a woman can uplift or bring down a man.

Indeed, you may have been enjoying the benefits of sexual energy transmutation even without knowing it. Reflect back to the epoch of your greatest and most worthy accomplishments and you will find that they occurred during the periods when you either enjoyed a harmonious sexual relationship, or you knowing or unknowingly refrained from excessive sexual indulgence - possibly because you were so focused and intent on achieving your goals that you forgot about sex for a while.

Sex, the carnal root of Man's *generation*, can be the source of his *degeneration*, yet holds the key to his *regeneration*; and when properly harnessed, the primordial powers of sex, and its creative essences that initiate all earthly existence, can be used to achieve anything you want. *Transmutation* is the key.

**OLD AGE
IS DIVINE**

At this stage of life, man must renounce worldliness and fully embrace spirituality, in readiness for a peaceful and triumphant exit through that inexorable door called death.

OLD AGE
Eon of Conservation

Old age is the age of wisdom and conservation. For some, physical and sometimes mental activities begin to slow down. In this concluding stage of man's earth life, sensual passions naturally begin to diminish, as wisdom enthrones and spirituality blossoms. A balanced youth life naturally portends a glorious and potentially divine old age.

At this stage of life, and having attained wealth and wisdom, man is inclined to generously giving back to humanity, not only his possessions but also his knowledge and wisdom, in appreciation for the good life he has enjoyed on earth.

At this stage of life, man must renounce worldliness and fully embrace spirituality, in readiness for a peaceful and triumphant exit through that inexorable door called death.

Napoleon Hill opines that a man reaches the zenith of his personal achievement between the ages of 40 and 60 years. This epoch also corresponds with the end of the *butterfly* years, and the beginning of a gradual but steady decline of his interest in un-planned sexual activities, and signals the onset of an involuntary but natural process of sexual energy sublimation.

Within this period, a man begins to align himself with societal responsibilities and expectations; and begins to focus his mental and emotional energies more on family and business, instead of the pursuit of transient sexual excitement. As a man exits from his youthful butterfly years, his sexual energy naturally begins to conserve and sublimate.

As man enters old age, there is a natural tendency toward sexual abstinence. This is Nature's benevolent way to help sustain the

---

**SEX IN
OLD AGE**

Excessive loss of semen, which is drawn from vital organs of the body can weaken or even shorten the life of an old man.

---

man's health and vitality - by reducing the urge for frequent depletion of life-force. Therefore the usual attempt by man to forcefully reverse a natural decline of sexual desire in old age with drugs and stimulants is really unnecessary.

At age sixty and beyond, a wise man should conserve his creative essence and deploy it to higher creative outlets. Excessive loss of semen, which is drawn from vital organs of the body, can weaken and even shorten the life of such a man.

If he must indulge in sex, then he should aim to enjoy love making without dissipating his vital life essence. Sexual techniques such as conscious retention and mutual absorption should be emphasized in old age.

Thankfully, as advanced old age sets in, a man can naturally abstain from sex for longer periods. The time it takes for him to recover from each physical release is much longer. This helps to conserve his life force, which protects, revitalizes and sustains the aging body.

THE SECRET OF
IMMORTALITY

The union of man and
woman is like the mating
of Heaven and Earth.

It is because of their
correct mating that
Heaven and Earth
last forever.

Humans have lost this
secret and have therefore
become mortal.

By knowing it the
path to immortality
is opened.

Shang-Ku-San-Tai

BALANCE
Nature's Way

Wise couples know the importance of maintaining balance in their sexual activities. There can be no hard and fast rule on sexual relationships. Each couple will establish their own pattern depending on their age, disposition and drive. How much sex is adequate, too much or too little is a private matter for individuals or couples to determine for themselves.

However, there is no disputing the fact that wise couples will nurture their relationship by maintaining a healthy balance between the giving and receiving of sexual pleasure and satisfaction. Any relationship driven by a selfish desire for personal gratification on the part of the man or the woman is in serious danger of eventual collapse.

Balance is Nature's way. The individual or couple must know where to draw the fine line of balance in their sexual activities. Couples should be happy and satisfied with their sex life; and the secret is to keep it balanced. At all times, caution and reason should prevail.

Most importantly, before couples enter into sexual intercourse, there should be mutual desire; or in the least, there must be mutual consent to give or receive sexual pleasure.

ALIGN YOUR LOVE AFFAIRS WITH THE RIGHT LUNAR INFLUENCE

By understanding the influence of the phases of the moon on the passion of woman, satisfaction can very easily be achieved. Without following these teachings, a person becomes liable to all kinds of sexual difficulties, such as love quarrels.

Ananga Ranga

SEX CYCLE
Benevolent Secret

Just like most activities in Nature, there is a most opportune time and season for sexual union between couples. Those who observe or *listen* to their body will notice that there are periods in the lunar cycle when the sex urge is stronger and in abundance; and there are periods when the sex urge is weaker and at low ebb.

This is due to the astrological influence of the moon on planet earth – the lunar cycle. However, lunar influence is not limited to sexual energy or desire alone. Some types of ailments such as mental disorder are known to aggravate and recede in accord with particular phases of the moon, hence the term *lunatic*.

By closely observing their sexual moods between new-moon and full-moon, couples can be able to know and appreciate how the different phases of the moon affect their sexual appetite and excitement.

The joys and pleasures of sexual intercourse

are greatly amplified when couples synchronize the purpose of their love making with the appropriate lunar influences. Right application of this secret promotes sexual satisfaction and harmonious relationship.

At the peak periods, usually full moon, the sexual passion or libido is greatly enhanced and more intense than at other times. In this same period too, the creative and spiritual energies in man are more intense and highly potent.

The discerning adept knows that the self-same upsurge in sexual desire can, simply by a switch of intent, become a super-surge in personal success in other areas of life, if properly harnessed.

> **LUNAR CYCLE**
>
> HE appointed the Moon for seasons; the Sun knoweth his going down.
>
> Psalm 104:19.

As man grows older, his craving for sexual contact begins to subside. With increased mental and spiritual advancement, he is better able to exert greater control over his sensual desires.

Progressively, the young man who some years back only had to think of the opposite sex to get excited now needs to see, touch or even feel her body, to get excited; and with further ascent into old age, may even require some external stimuli to do so. Gradually, *men-o-pause* sets in.

This is Nature's benevolent way to protect the man from excessive depletion of vital life-force required to keep him healthy and strong at old age.

Unfortunately, some men view this as a defect or weakness of their manhood and as such develop a complex about it; and they resort to stimulants and aphrodisiacs in a futile attempt to restore the virility of youth.

Except where medical attention is obviously required, attempting to reverse a natural decline of libido in old age is really unnecessary. As we grow old, our focus on sensual passions begins to subside, giving way to increased spirituality. This is really nothing to worry about, because it is a natural phenomenon.

THE BEST MEDICINE

Love-making, with a beautiful and generous woman, performed with careful attention, is the best medicine of all.

Sushruta Samhita

SEXUAL HEALING
The Best Medicine

There is superlative healing power in sex. When practiced correctly, sex can heal and rejuvenate the whole body – physically, emotionally and spiritually.

During sexual intercourse between couples, there are some quite noticeable changes in the breathing, heartbeat, blood circulation, perspiration and glandular secretions of both partners. Less noticeable but equally present are changes in emotional and brain wave energy. All these have varying effects on the whole body.

The efficacy of therapeutic love-making rests on the knowledge that some rhythmic movements and sexual positions, as well as certain postures and activities, produce and re-direct energy flows within the body of copulating partners.

Oriental medicine teaches that by adopting certain sexual positions, and controlling the rhythm and tempo of love-making, the therapeutic benefits of sexual intercourse can be obtained. The fundamental principle behind *sexual healing* is the circulation rather than dissipation of sexual energy.

Taoist teaching recognizes the important role of the woman in the generation of the restorative and healing powers of sex. She must wholly and happily surrender herself to her partner, giving sexual pleasure without reservations and receiving sexual pleasure without reservations. That way, she opens up her awesome powers of rejuvenation that has a limitless potential to heal both herself and her partner.

**SEXUAL
HEALING**

There is superlative healing power in sex. When correctly used, sex can heal and rejuvenate the whole body.

Intercourse postures and rhythms that naturally generate and circulate energy between the couples, must be emphasized, if sexual healing is to be achieved. There are several of these healing postures and rhythms; and their efficacy depends on the man's ability to control ejaculation, and the woman's readiness to circulate healing energy.

The hidden potency in sex as a source of mutual healing and rejuvenation can be experienced through wise and correct indulgence in sexual intercourse. Correct sexual experience can improve vitality, increase mental power, stabilize the emotions, and illumine the spirit.

A passionate, harmonious and balanced sex life promotes good health, creativity and productivity through a natural alignment of *mind and body*. Higher levels of sexual freedom and ecstasy can be attained when there is no inhibition or suppression of erotic feelings and fantasies by the couples.

Incorrect sexual practices deplete mental, spiritual, emotional and physical energy. Sex can bind, and sex can liberate the spirit of man.

AVOID FORCED EJACULATION

Every man should regulate the emission of semen according to his store of vital essence. He should never force himself to ejaculate. If he should do so, then his body will be harmed.

Taoist Wisdom

SEXUAL KILLING
Eating the Seed of Life

When sexual intercourse culminates in ejaculation by the man, there is a discharge of vital life-force which leaves the man temporarily de-magnetized; and if in excess, leaves him deflated. Such a man has eaten from the proverbial tree of life to the point where his body is depleted of every life-force and function. The power of sex to heal a man is not in doubt; but when incorrectly indulged in, sex can debilitate a man.

Recall the bible story of Samson and Delilah. With his *vital essence* completely depleted by the beautiful Delilah, Samson lost both his physical and mystical powers, and was captured by the Philistines. But while in their custody, his hair gradually grew back. In the *re-building* period required to sprout a half-grown hair, Samson was able to re-vitalize and restore his physical and mystical powers; and was thus able to pull down the main pillars of the stadium, killing himself and hundreds of spectators, to the eternal chagrin of the Philistines.

Excessive emission of semen weakens a man both physically and spiritually. This is because the offloaded semen must be replenished by drawing the vital ingredients that constitute semen from major organs and power centres of the body. And this restorative process takes awhile, depending on the age, health and vitality of the man.

> ### BE NOT GREEDY FOR
> ### FEMININE BEAUTY
>
> A man should learn to control his ejaculation. To be greedy for feminine beauty and emit beyond one's vigour injures every vein, nerve and organ in the body, and gives rise to every illness. Correct practice of sexual intercourse can cure every ailment and at the same time open the doors to Liberation.
>
> Yang-Sheng-Yao-Chi

Frequent or excessive loss of semen can seriously weaken the body's natural defence system, and thus expose a man to all forms of undesirable illnesses.

The decision to retain or ejaculate semen is a personal choice of the man; and this depends on his personal circumstances and objectives. Ejaculation should never be forced, especially when the man is sick, weak or in low spirit.

The wise wife or partner, while doing whatever she can to ensure that her man's attention is focused on herself, should avoid leading him to excessive emission of semen. The proverbial *milking him dry* is not only detrimental, but also quite unnecessary.

A successful sexual act should not always be judged by whether a man or his partner *comes* or does not come. There is much more to sexual union than to experience explosive and multiple orgasms.

Over-focusing on sex and its gratification will ultimately lead a man to dissipate his precious substance. The result is depletion of his mental powers, as well as his capacity to make contact with the higher life currents and vibrations of the Universe.

The result of excessive indulgence in sexual pleasure is pain, disease and ultimately, death. This is the price a man pays for unbridled enjoyment of life and his inability to rein-in the sensations of the flesh.

Research reveals that shortly after the euphoria of sexual conquest, the man begins to feels a sense of loss, depletion and depression; he becomes weak and irritable, and wants to be left alone. This negative feeling is detrimental to any creative effort, including wealth creation and accumulation of riches.

CONSCIOUS REGULATION

It is quite possible for a man to consciously regulate his ejaculations. When he is making love to a woman, he should ideally only release his semen two or three times in every ten sessions.

Master Tung

Over-indulgence in sex is detrimental, not only to the physical body but also to all forms of creativity. Depletion of sexual energy is tantamount to depletion of the creative potency in man.

Intuition is your ability to *know instinctively*. Imagination is your ability to *see it in your head*. To be successful, and to rise above mediocrity, a man must fully avail himself of his own powers of intuition and creative imagination.

Incessant waste of life-force results in slow but steady disintegration of the body, and ultimately, death. Conservation is key to regeneration, vitality and youthfulness.

Taoist wisdom teaches that a man's supply of the *yang-essence* is finite. Therefore, it must be jealously conserved. Excessive ejaculation of semen, man's vital life-force, is detrimental to the human system - mentally, emotionally and spiritually, and should be avoided.

Life is all about balance. Everything has its use, place and purpose in the divine plan. Therefore Man, as the key player and master of his earthly destiny, must align with and uphold this divine plan. Moderation is the key to vitality and power. The wise man controls and conserves his vital force.

FORCED MATERNITY

No words can express the helplessness, the sense of personal desecration, the despair which sinks into the heart of a woman forced to submit to maternity under adverse circumstances, and when her own soul rejects it. Man, in begetting a child without regards to the wishes and condition of his wife, heedless of the physical and spiritual well being of his offspring, commits the greatest outrage any human being can perpetrate on another. Motherhood should be a privilege and an opportunity, not a penalty or misfortune.

H. C. Wright

PROCREATION
Highest Creative Power

Biological procreation begins with fulfilment of sexual desire. For the wise couple, the procreative process begins with a well planned sexual communion - *the outward ritual of a spiritual process* through which human souls sojourn to mother earth to experience life.

Procreation is therefore an act of great spiritual responsibility, which begins as the desire to propagate and perpetuate oneself on earth.

The enlightened couple will do well to avoid unplanned or forced procreation. Sadly, most conceptions today occur without the mutual consent of one or both partners; and this does more harm than good to both the foetus and the mother.

A fleeting moment of sensual *enjoyment* whose consequence compels a would-be mother to bear nine months of pregnancy that gives her little or no joy; and forces a foetus to absorb nine months of cursing and anger from an unhappy mother to be, is better avoided.

For the wise couple therefore, the bringing of an offspring into the world should be by choice, not by chance. When such a couple desires and decides to procreate, and before they enter into the procreative communion, they should follow certain procedures to prepare and harmonize themselves, not just physically, but also mentally, emotionally and spiritually. That way, they are sure to attract unto themselves a baby *angel* with the qualities they have prayed for.

> **MAN'S UTMOST
> CREATIVE POWER**
>
> As the singular act through which Man expresses his highest creative power of bringing offspring into the world, sexual intercourse is much more than mere physical conjugation; it is an act of great responsibility, with deep spiritual and mystical connotations.

Such couples must be truly in love, in good health and in high spirits. All negative emotions such as anger, envy, fear and revenge must be banished from their minds, and replaced with thoughts of love, peace and harmony.

Before the procreative union, the couple may observe a short period of sexual fast, during which time they focus on the qualities they desire in their new-born baby. A moderate sexual fast increases desire, potency and virility.

During the procreative communion, the couples should endeavour to keep their thoughts focused on each other, so that their offspring may resemble or take after them. If during the procreative communion any of the partners indulges in imaginative adultery, the offspring may take after the personality imagined.

At the appropriate time, the couple must embark on this all important mission with care, love and wisdom, fully aware that their sexual union is the genesis of the coming of another human soul unto the world; and with the understanding that their union shall be fruitful and a blessing, not only to them but to all mankind.

Couples should always adopt such suitable positions for sexual intercourse that meet their intended purpose or sexual fantasy. For procreation, the man-on-top position is ideal as it allows full and deep penetration of the penis into the vagina, which ensures that the semen, assisted by gravity, is deposited as close as possible to the entrance of the womb. This improves the possibility for conception and allows the couples to adore and appreciate each other's endowments as they perform their sacred duty.

A WHOLESOME DIET PROMOTES FERTILITY

A wholesome diet promotes healthy physical and spiritual growth in a person. Indulgence in an unwholesome diet produces disease and worldly problems.

Sushruta Samhita

Equipped with better understanding of sexual secrets, intending couples become empowered to make intelligent and well planned expression and execution of their highest creative mandate – the bringing of new life unto earth.

Under optimum conditions of love, mutual consent, harmony and free flow of creative energy, the couples are sure beget ideal souls in perfectly formed bodies, unto planet earth.

**NOTHING
IS NEW**

I have nothing new
to teach the world.

Truth and Non-violence
are as old as the hills.

All I have done is to try
experiments in both on
as vast a scale as I could.

Mahatma Gandhi

LAST LINES
Man Know Thyself

Man is naturally imbued with potent creative energy. Through Mind action this energy can convert from one form to another.

Thought is creative energy, and you may chose to focus it on sex or on whatever else you want; and that determines your result.

Man creates through his Thoughts held in Mind. Desires and Ideas stimulate *mental activity*. Given enough stimuli, this invisible creative energy ultimately brings forth its physical equivalent.

Whatever a man passionately desires and ideates, he attracts. Thus any thought held in Mind long enough, comes to fruition. That way, man creates his *World* and predicts his own *Future*.

Spirit essence is everywhere present, potent and operative. As a spiritual being, Man is under the authority and compulsion of Spirit. Therefore Man's primary constituency is spirituality. When Spirit enthrones and takes full dominion in Man, his *Mind* is at peace, his *Body* is harmonized, and his *Affairs* are ordered.

Semen is man's most precious possession, harbouring all his creative essences. Its constituents are drawn from major organs of the body. These same major organs are associated with or linked to the major energy centres of the body.

Excessive emission of semen de-vitalizes, deflates and de-magnetizes the man; but if conserved, it sublimates and strengthens the power centres, especially the Crown.

Depletion of man's creative essence through excessive emission is detrimental to all forms of creativity - including the creation of wealth and the accumulation of riches.

To rise above mediocrity, a man must avail himself of his powers of *creative imagination* - the faculty of spiritual increase. Excessive sexual indulgence depletes this faculty.

A well nourished brain expands your mental capacity for higher levels of cerebral activity. With a tremendous brain power comes also acumen, perception, intuition, zeal and dogged determination - the basic primary constituents for success in any endeavour.

Joy is the ultimate purpose of all striving. We all want to be joyful - that great feeling that comes with attainment of our heart's desire. Joy is an inside emotion activated by the successful or progressive attainment of our dreams, visions and desires.

Your natural gifts and talents determine and shape your channel of service to the world, which ultimately gives you satisfaction, and brings you joy. You'll experience satisfaction and joy that passeth all understanding when your service channel to the world aligns with your *calling,* and the true purpose of all life - to express GOD on earth.

Back of dreams and visions is life-purpose. Discovering your purpose gives you focus and evolves your *life-path*; a path that leads to the success which ultimately brings you the fulfilment, contentment and joy you desire and deserve.

When you discover your *true-self* and life purpose; when you hook-up to your genuine *mandate* on earth, you begin to *dream* with your eyes open and you start to *see* with your eyes closed. Your energies begin to conserve, intensify and surge, as all your thoughts and actions converge on your one and only goal - to reach the top of your Mount Everest, whatever it is.

When you activate your energy centres, you empower yourself with the creative ability to serve humanity in whatever capacity or calling you love and enjoy.

Life is all about service. *Service* is the channel through which you add *Value* to the world, and for which the world rewards and honours you. The greater your *value-added* to the world, the higher your reward.

Service is your sure channel of blessings. Therefore discover your *calling*, evolve your *service-path* and set your mind to serve diligently and receive gratefully.

Discover your talents, gifts and abilities and put then to work - they are your *open doors* that no one can close. This hen that lays golden eggs hibernates in you right now; awaken it and put it to work. Use what you have to get what you want!

You'll surely make speedy progress on your chosen service-path or *life-work* when you eschew bitterness, anger and envy. Such negative and destructive emotions constrict your channels of blessings and restrict your open doors. Always forgive and move on.

Do away with the *victim* mentality and adopt a *response-ability* approach to whatever happens in your life. Accepting responsibility and taking requisite action empowers you to take your earthly destiny in your own hands, whatever the situation.

Develop a positive mental attitude by living a life of gratitude and positive expectancy; firmly holding your *cup* upright under the fount of in-exhaustible cosmic flow of love and wisdom that lead you to success in all your undertakings.

That way, you keep your open doors open, and your channels of blessings flowing; and you are sure to receive abundant *goodness and plenty*, as you dwell perpetually in the constant flow of divine substance. *Namaste!*

MY LIFE IS
A DREAM

My *Life* is
like a dream;
and I look forward to
waking up one day,
on the other side
of the great *Veil*,
and looking back
to say:

*Wao! What a
beautiful dream!*

Jay Onwukwe

The Author

A graduate of the University of Reading, UK, and the University of Nigeria, Enugu, Jay Onwukwe holds first degrees in Estate Management; and in Surveying and Geodesy.

His professional career of over twenty years as a geophysical seismic surveyor involved field operations and duty tours into remote and mostly unexplored terrains of Sudan, Yemen, the Chad Basin and Niger Delta, while working for multi-national oil companies.

Those regular trips into Mother Nature in its pure nakedness, and the consequent abstinence from regular social interactions and activities, not only kindled his interest in, but also empowered his study into the innate powers of Man and Nature.

Jay is a friend of Youths. His earlier work - **The WEALTH SECRETS You Must Know Before40** - is a best-selling knowledge book available at Amazon, and a must-read for every aspiring youth.

He enjoys reading, writing and gardening of rare and exotic plants.

Selected
Bibliography

Alice B. Stockham M.D., *Karezza: Ethics of Marriage*, 1903.

Dr. Bernard Jensen, *Love, Sex & Nutrition*
Avery Pub. Group, 1988.

Grigson G., *The Goddess Of Love: The Birth, Death And Return of Aphrodite*
Constable, London, 1976.

John Humphrey Noyes, *Male Continence*
Oneida N. Y., 1872.

John Muirhead-Gould (Editor), *The Kama Sutra Of Vatsyayana*, 1963.

J. William Lloyd, *Magnetation: The Art of Connubial Love*
Roscoe Calif., 1931.

Manly Hall, *The Secret Teachings of All Ages*
Los Angeles, 1973.

Napoleon Hill, *Think And Grow Rich*
     Wilshire Book Company, 1966.

Nik Douglas and Penny Slinger, *Sexual Secrets: The Alchemy of Ecstasy*
     Arrow Books, 1982.

Made in the USA
San Bernardino, CA
17 November 2016